Beetles

Beetles

Peter Murray

THE CHILD'S WORLD®

Published in the United States of America by The Child's World®
P.O. Box 326
Chanhassen, MN 55317-0326
800-599-READ
www.childsworld.com

Project Manager Mary Berendes
Editor Katherine Stevenson, Ph.D.
Designer Mary Berendes
**Our sincere thanks to Robert Mitchell, Ph.D.,
for his input and guidance on this book.**

Photo Credits
© 1993 Adam Jones/Dembinsky Photo Assoc. Inc.: 6
ANIMALS ANIMALS © Bill Beatty: 15, 29 (main)
ANIMALS ANIMALS © Bruce Davidson: 10
ANIMALS ANIMALS © George Bryce: 24, 29 (inset)
ANIMALS ANIMALS © Jack Clark: 19
ANIMALS ANIMALS © OSF/COOKE, J.A.L.: 20 (inset)
© Mark Moffett/Minden Pictures: 20 (main)
© Michael P. Gadomski/Photo Researchers, Inc.: 26
© M. L. Jameson/University of Nebraska State Museum: 30
© Robert & Linda Mitchell: cover, 2, 9, 13, 16, 23

Library of Congress Cataloging-in-Publication Data
Murray, Peter, 1952 Sept. 29–
Beetles / by Peter Murray.
p. cm.
ISBN 1-56766-976-X (lib. bdg. : alk. paper)
1. Beetles—Juvenile literature. [1. Beetles.] I. Title.
QL576.2 .M87 2003
595.76—dc21
2001000301

On the cover...

Front cover: This grapevine beetle is sitting on a flower in Texas.
Page 2: This longhorned beetle lives in a jungle in Borneo.

Table of Contents

There is a kind of creature that lives almost everywhere. Turn over just about any rock and you can find them underneath. You can find them hiding under the bark of trees. You can find them swimming in ponds. You can find them eating the vegetables in your garden. The more you look, the more of these creatures you will find. What are they? They're beetles!

⇐ This milkweed beetle is resting on a milkweed plant.

What Are Beetles?

Beetles are a kind of **insect**. The body of an adult insect is divided into three different areas. The front area is the head. The middle area is the **thorax**, or chest. The back area is the **abdomen**, or stomach region. All insects have two eyes, two feelers (called **antennae**), and six legs. Most insects also have two sets of wings.

Beetles are different from other insects because their front wings are hard. These wings work like armor to protect the beetle's softer thorax, rear wings, and abdomen.

Here you can see the hard outer wings (brown with yellow ⇒ spots) and soft inner wings of this longhorned beetle.

Are There Different Kinds of Beetles?

There are more than 300,000 different kinds, or **species**, of beetles. In fact, one out of every five animals on Earth is a beetle. Each species is different in its own way. *Lady beetles* (also called *ladybugs*) are small, reddish orange beetles with black spots. *Rhinoceros beetles* have long horns they use for fighting each other. *Stag beetles* have huge pointed jaws and can grow to be over three inches long. Adult *goliath beetles* can be eight inches long—big enough to cover your face!

⇐ This goliath beetle is crawling on a man's hand in Africa.

Beetles live in almost every part of the world. They live in rainy jungles and dry deserts. They make their homes on the ground, in trees, in the water, and even underground! About the only places you won't find beetles are the North and South Poles, where the weather is too cold for them.

Beautiful six-spotted scarab beetles like ⇒ this one live in the jungles of Malaysia.

What Are Baby Beetles Like?

Like most insects, beetles hatch from eggs. They do not look like their parents right away. Instead, the newly hatched **larvae** look like little worms. The larvae are very hungry and grow quickly. As they grow, they **molt**, or shed their skin, several times.

Next the babies turn into **pupae** for a few days or months. The pupae rest in a safe, quiet place and do not eat. During their rest, the pupae change into their adult shapes and grow wings. Finally the pupae molt one last time—but this time an adult beetle comes out of the old skin! This change from egg to adult is called **metamorphosis**.

Here you can see all four life stages of a Mexican ⇒ bean beetle: (1) eggs (2) larva (3) pupa (4) adult.

Different kinds of adult beetles eat different foods. *Tiger beetles* catch and eat smaller insects. Goliath and stag beetles drink plant juices. Lady beetles help farmers and gardeners by eating insects that damage flowers and other plants.

But not all beetles are so helpful. *Snout beetles* (also called *weevils*) are pests to farmers because they eat crops. *Asian longhorned beetles* damage trees as they chew their way through them. *Japanese beetles* destroy fruit trees, rose bushes, corn plants, soybean plants, and shade trees.

⇐ This acorn weevil is feeding on an oak acorn.

Beetle larvae are always hungry. They need food to help them grow and develop. Beetle larvae eat anything from crops and flowers to other insects. Some larvae eat even stranger things. *Carpet beetles* live in people's homes. They lay their eggs in cracks in the floor under carpets and furniture. When the eggs hatch, the hungry larvae eat almost anything they can find—feather pillows, wallpaper paste, insulation, and even hot red-pepper powder!

Dung beetle larvae hatch from eggs in the middle of a buried ball of dung. The larvae eat the dung until they are ready to dig their way to the surface.

Here you can see the larva of a carpet beetle. ⇒

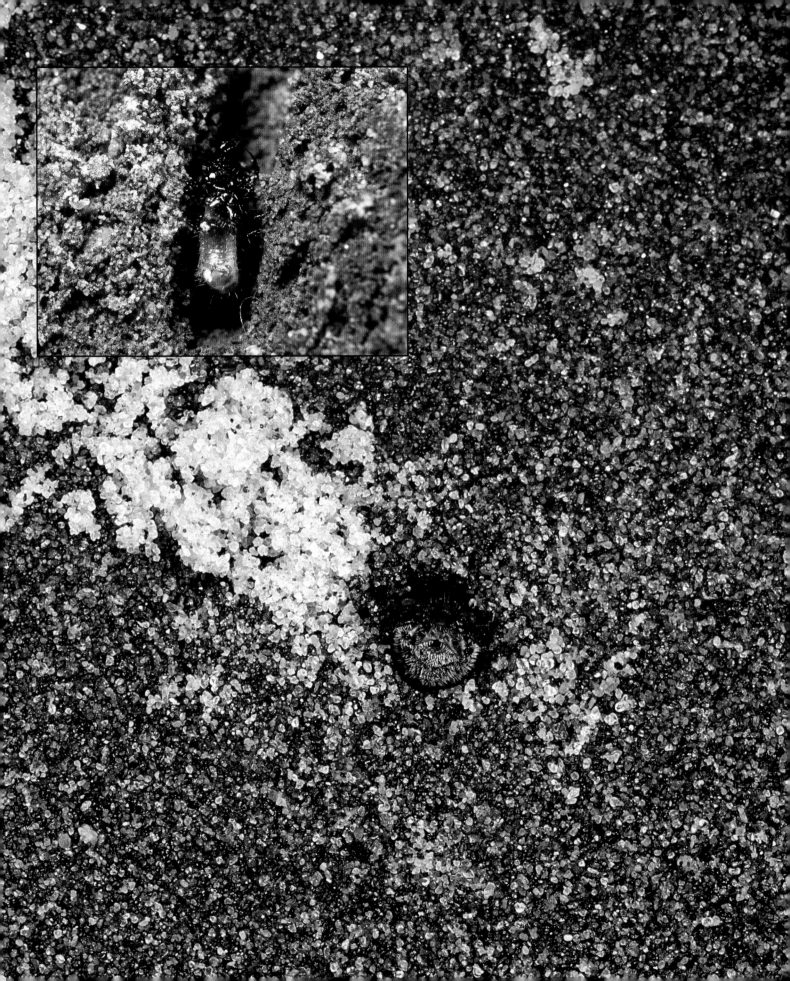

Tiger beetle larvae eat other insects. They also have an interesting way of catching them. The larvae live in holes. Only their large jaws show above the ground. When other insects pass by, the larvae reach out and grab them.

Once the larvae are fully grown, they dig deeper into the ground and slowly change into their adult form. They shed their skin, grow wings, and return to the surface as adults.

⇐ *Main photo*: Just the jaws of this Northeastern beach tiger beetle larva can be seen above the ground.

Small photo: This is what a tiger beetle larva looks like inside the ground.

Do Beetles Have Enemies?

Birds, frogs, spiders, snakes, fish, and even other insects find beetles to be a tasty treat. In fact, when farmers have trouble with beetles, they sometimes simply bring in another insect to eat them!

About 75 years ago, Japanese beetles were eating too many crops in the United States. Scientists found another insect that could help control the beetles—the *spring Tiphia wasp*. The wasps' young love to eat young Japanese beetles. They help keep the Japanese beetles under control.

This adult Tiphia wasp is resting on a leaf in Texas. ⇒

Beetles have many tricks for protecting themselves. *Bombardier beetles* are the skunks of the beetle world. When attacked by an enemy, the bombardier beetle fights back. With a loud popping sound, the beetle shoots out a hot, bad-smelling liquid. A puff of smoke even billows from the beetle's abdomen! If you were an enemy, you would think twice before trying to eat a bombardier beetle again!

⇐ Here you can see a bombardier beetle as it crawls on a beach.

Many beetles are helpless if turned on their backs—but not the *click beetle*! If it is threatened, it rolls onto its back and pretends to be dead. After the enemy leaves, the beetle bends its body and snaps it back with a loud "click!" The beetle flips into the air and back onto its feet.

The *eyed click beetle* has another trick. It uses **mimicry** to fool attackers. Huge spots on its thorax look like big eyes. Hungry birds and frogs think the spots are the eyes of a larger animal and pass the beetle by.

⇐ This Eastern eyed click beetle is crawling on a log in a Pennsylvania forest. You can see the eyelike markings on its back.

Are Beetles Dangerous?

Most beetles aren't dangerous to people at all. But some beetles, such as *blister beetles*, should be avoided. Blister beetles have a liquid in their bodies that can cause blisters on your skin. Stag beetles can also be dangerous. Their large jaws can pinch if you're not careful. But for the most part, beetles are harmless. They simply want to eat, lay their eggs, and be left alone.

Main photo: From close up, it is easy to see how the ⇒ jaws of a stag beetle like this one could be dangerous.

Small photo: This picture shows a blister beetle pretending to be dead. The shiny liquid on its legs could cause blisters to people who touch it.

Even though there are countless beetles in the world, some species are in danger of dying out. They are in danger because the places where they live are being destroyed. *Wingless dung beetles, broad-toothed stag beetles,* and *American burying beetles* are just three types that have very low numbers.

Insects are the most numerous creatures on the planet, and beetles are among the most successful and widespread. There are surely many kinds of beetles that haven't even been discovered yet, especially in the world's rain forests. Beetles are an important and fascinating part of the world around us. The next time you are out in your yard or a park, see how many different types of beetles you can spot. You might be surprised!

← Here you can see a rare American burying beetle as it crawls on a dead rat.

Glossary

abdomen (AB-doh-men)
An insect's abdomen is its stomach area. Beetles have an abdomen.

antennae (an-TEN-nee)
Antennae are the long feelers on an insect's head. Beetles use their antennae to help them find food.

insect (IN-sekt)
An insect is an animal that has three body areas, six legs, and one or two pairs of wings. Beetles are insects.

larvae (LAR-vee)
Larvae are young insects between the egg stage and the pupa stage of life. Beetle larvae look like little worms.

metamorphosis (meh-tuh-MOR-fuh-siss)
Metamorphosis is a series of changes some animals go through from egg to adult. Beetles go through metamorphosis.

mimicry (MIM-ik-ree)
Mimicry is the ability to look or act like something else. The big "eyes" on eyed click beetles are a kind of mimicry that keeps the beetles safe.

molt (MOLT)
When an animal molts, it sheds its outer layer of skin, fur, or feathers.

pupae (PYOO-pee)
Pupae are young insects that are not quite adults yet. Beetle pupae rest while their bodies change into their adult shapes.

species (SPEE-sheez)
A species is a different kind of an animal. There are more than 300,000 different species of beetles.

thorax (THOR-ax)
An insect's thorax is its chest area. Beetles have a thorax.

Web Sites

Visit our homepage for lots of links about beetles!

http://www.childsworld.com/links.html

Note to Parents, Teachers, and Librarians:
We routinely verify our Web links to make sure they're safe, active sites—so encourage your readers to check them out!

Index